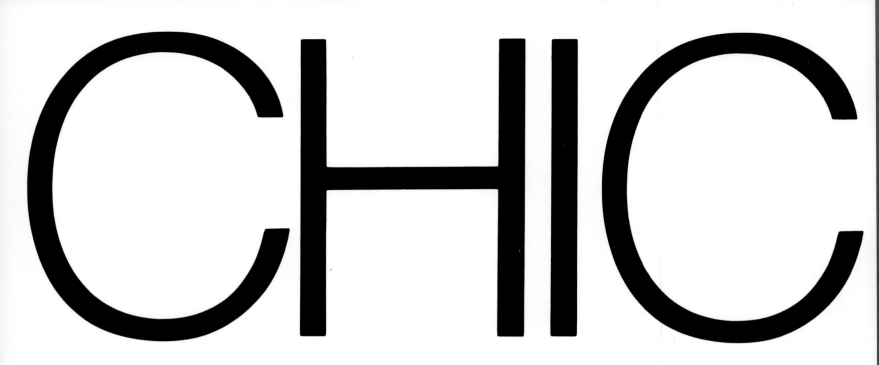

CHIC

CONTENTS

Published by Gallery Books
A Division of W H Smith Publishers Inc.
112 Madison Avenue
New York, New York 10016

Produced by
Brompton Books Corp.
15 Sherwood Place
Greenwich, CT 06830

ISBN 0-8317-1252-X

Printed in Hong Kong

10 9 8 7 6 5 4 3 2

AGO

TEXT	THOMAS G AYLESWORTH VIRGINIA L AYLESWORTH
PHOTOGRAPHY	MARCELLO BERTINETTI ANGELA WHITE BERTINETTI
DESIGN	RICHARD GLASSMAN

GALLERY BOOKS
An imprint of W.H. Smith Publishers Inc.
112 Madison Avenue
New York, New York 10016

Acknowledgments

The authors and publisher would like to thank the following people who have helped in the preparation of this book: Richard Glassman, who designed it; Robin Langley Sommer, who edited it; Mary R Raho, who did the picture research.

Photo Credits

All photographs by Marcello and Angela Bertinetti, with the following exceptions:
Sol Benjamin: 90
Chicago Convention and Tourism Bureau: 24, 49.
FPG International: 43, 46-47, 48 (above), 111. 114, 116,
Archie Lieberman: 97.
Françoise Robert: 40
Ron Schramm: 20-21, 25, 33, 34, 36-37, 41, 42, 69, 72-73, 74 (left), 85, 88, 89, 102, 109 (above), 113, 117, 121, 122-123, 125.

Preface

'Behold! She stands beside her inland sea.'

That's the beginning of the song that we learned in elementary school. And an inland sea it is. Lake Michigan is five times larger than the entire state of Connecticut; Switzerland and Luxembourg would disappear in it without a trace and still leave room to sink Rhode Island, Delaware and four cities the size of Los Angeles. Chicago is the jewel on Lake Michigan, facing the lake from the west and stretching more than 20 miles along its shore. And the lake, in turn, is the city's showcase, with a superb chain of parks and parkways flanking the shore and the city's tallest and finest buildings rising behind them.

Chicago, the metropolis of the Midwest, is not an old city like Boston, New York or St Augustine. But long before the first white settlers arrived, the Chicago area was important to transportation. The Indians used it as a portage, carrying their canoes from the Des Plaines River to the Chicago River, then paddling them to Lake Michigan. Possibly the first white men to use the Chicago portage were Louis Joliet and Father Jacques Marquette, two French explorers. This was in 1673, on their way to what is now Green Bay, Wisconsin. Marquette and two companions camped near the Chicago River in the winter of 1674-75.

But the first permanent settler was the black man Jean Baptiste Point du Sable, who established a trading post on the north bank of the river in 1779. The Indians controlled the area until 1794, when General 'Mad Anthony' Wayne defeated them in the Battle of Fallen Timbers, and the Indians ceded to the United States 'One piece of land Six Miles Square at the mouth of the Chicakgo River.' There is an argument about what 'Chicakgo' or, more correctly, 'Checagou' means. No one doubts that it was an Indian word, but some historians say it meant 'skunk' or 'wild onion,' both of which are still fairly common in the area; others think it meant 'big,' 'great' or 'powerful.' It probably depends on how one feels about the city.

Some people also call it 'the Windy City,' but no one knows who coined that phrase. Carl Sandburg called it 'the City of the Big Shoulders.' A J Liebling, a New York writer, called it 'the Second City.' Songwriters called it 'That Toddlin' Town.' Boosters called it 'the City That Works.' Frank Sinatra sang of it as 'My Kind of Town.' More than 3 million people call it 'Home.' And the 31 percent of the United States population who live within 500 miles of this metropolis call it 'the City.' Since 1818, wherever one looks in Chicago, it lives up to its motto, 'I Will.'

Chicago had a tough time before it became a city in that year of 1818. Soldiers built Fort Dearborn in 1803, and by 1812 a small settlement had grown up nearby. But the Federal Government abandoned the outpost in the war of 1812, and the Indians massacred the settlers and burned the fort. It wasn't until 1816 that Fort Dearborn was rebuilt, and the settlement became a village two years later. Its boundaries weren't defined until 1830, when a commission mapped a proposed canal from Ottawa, to the west, to Chicago, to the east, and laid out both towns. It wasn't until 1833 that Chicago was incorporated as a town. It became a city in 1837, with a population of only 4000—but it was the seat of Cook County.

The growth of the city probably began in 1848, when the Illinois and Michigan Canal was completed, giving farmers to the west a chance to ship their products to the east by way of Lake Michigan. Between 1848 and 1850, Chicago's population went from 20,000 to 30,000. Then in 1856 the Galena and Chicago Union Railroad began operating, and Chicago's place as a transportation center was assured. By 1860, the year that Abraham Lincoln was nominated for president in Chicago, the city had 112,172 residents. By 1870, almost 300,000 people were living in the city.

Then came the great Chicago Fire in 1871, and the entire business district was wiped out. The fire raged for more than 24 hours, destroying 17,450 buildings and razing some 3-1/3 square miles of the city. At least 300 people were killed, 90,000 were left homeless and $200 million dollars worth of property was lost.

It was then that 'I Will' became a reality. The people of the city spat on their hands and rebuilt. So well did they do the job that a mere 19 years later there were more than one million people living in Chicago—making it the nation's second largest city, second only to New York. In a way, the fire, tragic though it was, might have been a good thing for the city. Many of the slums were burned out, and the world's first skyscraper, the Home Insurance Building, was erected. Parks along the lake were planned. The downtown area came over the years from a dream to a reality. In 1893, just 22 years after the tragedy, Chicago held the World's Columbian Exposition on the South Side—a World's Fair celebrating the four-hundredth anniversary of the discovery of America by Christopher Columbus. Chicago had come back and was well on its way to being the gem of the prairie—the city of varied ethnic groups, artists, writers and architects.

Today, Chicago is certainly 'the City That Works.' It is the world's greatest railway center. Its O'Hare International Airport is the world's busiest, with some 65,000 take-offs and landings per year. More than 500 truck and bus lines are based in Chicago. It is the nation's leading wholesale distributing center, with its Chicago Board of Trade, where 90 percent of the country's contracts for delivery of grains are made; its Chicago Mercantile Exchange, which is the busiest market for farm products; its preponderance of America's largest mail-order houses.

It is a beautiful city, too, with its Magnificent Mile shopping area on North Michigan Avenue, its famous skyline, its 131 forest preserves, 572 city parks, 35 museums and 31 beaches.

People of all nationalities live in Chicago. It is still true that in Chicago you can get the best bratwurst outside Germany, the best kielbasa outside Poland, the best spanikopita outside Greece, the best pizza outside Naples and the best chiles rellenos outside Mexico. We still remember the stand on the corner where the hot dogs came with mustard, chopped tomatoes, cole slaw and chopped onions. We are still Cub fans and Bear fans, and we never call it 'Chi.' As the old song ended, 'My Heart is in Chicago wherever I may roam.'

Thomas G Aylesworth
Virginia L Aylesworth

The City Beautiful

Chicago is the city beautiful. Even with its towering skyscrapers, it never gives the feeling that is so common in New York—the hemmed-in feeling—the feeling that the buildings will fall at any minute—the feeling that the sun will never shine on the street. The streets and avenues are so wide, the sidewalks so spacious, that the feeling is almost like walking on a broad boulevard among monuments.

Michigan Avenue is undoubtedly the showcase of the downtown area. Near the Loop—the business core of Chicago, so-called because it is ringed by the elevated railroad tracks—it is a wide street with magnificent old buildings, including the Chicago Public Library, on the west, and on the east, except for a few fine buildings such as the Art Institute, the beautiful expanse of Grant Park. Going north on Michigan, after one passes the Chicago River, is the Magnificent Mile, containing some of the finest and largest stores in the country, as well as elegant hotels and office buildings.

Near the end of the Magnificent Mile is the Water Tower, at the corner of Michigan and Chicago Avenues. This was one of the few buildings to survive the great fire of 1871.

It was near the spot where Michigan Avenue crosses the river that Fort Dearborn was located, and that area, of course, was where Chicago began.

Grant Park stands between Michigan Avenue and the lake. This park is 'Chicago's front yard,' and in it are the Chicago Natural History Museum (formerly the Field Museum of Natural History), the John G Shedd Aquarium, the Alder Planetarium and Soldier Field, the enormous home of the Chicago Bears of the National Football League. During the summer, free concerts, from pops to classics, are held in the park.

17 Looking north from the Michigan Avenue bridge to the home of one of the most powerful and influential newspapers in the country—the Chicago Tribune—a rare example of the use of Gothic design for a modern skyscraper.

19 Chicago's wide streets stretch for miles, and the city planners have not forgotten the refreshing spots of greenery.

20/21 Chicago Harbor—the beautiful recreation area for yachtsmen—lies at the edge of Grant Park, almost in the shadows of the buildings that make up the city's lovely skyline.

22/23 Michigan Avenue looking north toward the Wrigley Building. The white Spanish-Renaissance-style structure was built in two sections, connected by a bridge at the third floor. The four-faced clock is two stories high.

24 Beautiful flowers form a stunning pattern near the botanical conservatory in Lincoln Park. Also in this park is Chicago's oldest zoo, a tiny farm to visit and the small but striking museum of the Chicago Academy of Sciences.

25 A view from Grant Park, with its intriguing statuary, toward the Conrad Hilton Hotel on South Michigan Avenue. With its 2279 rooms, the Hilton is one of the largest hostelries in the world.

26 Approaching the heart of the city on Lake Shore Drive, the highway that runs along the lake. Chicago was the birthplace of the skyscraper—an odd thing, since Chicago was built on sand, rather than granite, as was New York.

27 A view of the Wrigley Building looking across the Michigan Avenue Bridge, which crosses the Chicago River, famous as the river that flows backward. Engineers reversed its flow to prevent polluting Lake Michigan.

28/29 A panoramic view of Chicago Harbor and its marina. The tall building on the left is Sears Tower. At 1454 feet, it is the tallest building in the world. The 110-story office building has an observatory—open till midnight.

30 Clogged with traffic though it may be, Michigan Avenue is a pedestrian thorough-fare becaues of its wide sidewalks—a view looking north toward the Prudential Building (center).

31 To the north of the river on Michigan Avenue is the Old Water Tower—that quaint, architecturally ugly, fortress-like, wonderful building that is such a reminder of Chicago's past, before the fire. It has recently been restored inside to house a walk-in visitor's information center.

The City of the Arts

Learning about the arts was easy for a kid in Chicago in the good old days. There were the free children's concerts by the Chicago Symphony (where conductor Frederick Stock would say 'Everybody cough—blow your noses, and then we'll play,'), and the Grant Park Concerts. The great museums were either free or didn't charge admission on the days when school was out. The architecture of the Wrigley Building, Tribune Tower, the Board of Trade, Marshall Field's, Carson Pirie Scott's and the Merchandise Mart were familiar sights.

Come to think of it, the arts are readily accessible today. The present Chicago Symphony is arguably the best orchestra in the world. The theater is thriving. The museums are still wonderful—the Art Institute, the Museum of Science and Industry, the Museum of Natural History, the Shedd Aquarium, the Adler Planetarium, the Oriental Institute, the Lincoln Park Zoo, the Brookfield Zoo.

But perhaps it is the architecture that is the most striking thing about the city. Of course it was the birthplace of the modern skyscraper and the modern drawbridge. Even if it is a city of neat brick and wood cottages and bulky stone mansions, it produced the geniuses of the Chicago School of Architecture—Louis Sullivan, Daniel Burnham, Dankmar Adler, to name but three, whose innovative tradition was carried on by Frank Lloyd Wright and Ludwig Mies van der Rohe.

Finally, it has long been a writer's town. If fact, there once was a unique style of journalism in Chicago, as characterized in the play *The Front Page*, by Charles MacArthur and Ben Hecht. The roll call of Chicago writers is impressive—Saul Bellow, Carl Sandburg, Studs Terkel, Nelson Algren, James T Farrell, Jane Addams and many more.

33 Nowhere but Chicago can a sightseer encounter so much outdoor modern sculpture. Chicagoans either love it or shrug it off—there is still plenty of room on the sidewalk.

35 Marina City on North State Street is a condominium and commercial building complex with marina and boat storage. Designed by Bertrand Goldberg and Associates, it is one of the most unusual downtown living-working complexes in the United States.

36/37 The Four Seasons, an architectural mosaic by Marc Chagall—located in the First National Bank Plaza.

38/39 Part of the facade of the Chicago Tribune Tower.

40 Part of the facade of the Carson Pirie Scott & Company building on the corner of State and Madison Streets in the Loop. Louis Sullivan was the architect of this department store structure with its distinctive grillework and rich ornamentation on the first and second floors.

41 Marshall Field's Department Store—a landmark on State Street for more than one hundred years, and, its customers think, the best store in the world. Its famous clock projects over the sidewalk.

42 Another outdoor sculpture—Large Interior Form by Henry Moore.

43 The most famous outdoor sculpture of all: the Picasso sculpture in the Richard J Daley Plaza.

44 An evening concert in the James C Petrillo Music Shell in Grant Park.

45 The Art Institute of Chicago in Grant Park was founded in 1879 and now houses a world-renowned collection of American, European, Classical and Oriental art. A junior museum, an art school and the Goodman Theater are here.

46/47 Alexander Calder's Flamingo *in the Federal Center Plaza.*

48 top *The Museum of Science and Industry in Jackson Park—simply the finest museum of its kind in the world. Among its hundreds of exhibits, many of them providing visitor participation, are a coal mine, a captured German U-Boat, a miniature circus with 22,000 hand-carved pieces and the Colleen Moore Fairy Castle.*

48 bottom *The Field Museum of Natural History is one of the largest museums of its type in the world. It has a world-famous collection of primitive art, exhibits of Indian, Chinese and Tibetan cultures, geological exhibits and wonderful bird and animal habitat groups.*

49 Batcolumn *by Claes Oldenburg. Chicagoans loved it or hated it, but they knew what it was meant to be—an amulet for the Cubs and Sox.*

48

The City of People

Chicago is a city of people—people of all walks of life, people from every country in the world, people speaking dozens of different languages—but they are all Chicagoans. Time was when the city was a maze of ethnic enclaves. When the Germans came, they settled on the Near North Side. The Scandinavians went to the Northwest Side, the Greeks to South Halsted Street, the Poles to the West Side, the Southern blacks to the South Side, the Chinese to the Near South Side, and so on.

Today those sections are disappearing, since only about 12 out of every 100 Chicagoans were born in another country. Indeed, about the only real ethnic neighborhoods left are Chinatown, centering at Wentworth Street and Cermak Road, and Greek Town, on Halsted Street from Madison to Van Buren. But the best ethnic restaurants can still be found where the old neighborhoods used to be.

Chicago's people are always confident that something good is about to happen—and it usually does. Chicago has risen from the ashes more than once. There was the fire, and then there was the struggle faced by vast numbers of immigrants. Jane Addams, the founder of Hull House and winner of the Nobel Peace Prize, said, 'The older and richer inhabitants ... move away. They make room for the newly arrived immigrants, who are densely ignorant of civic duties. Meanwhile, the wretched conditions persist.' Today, the descendents of these downtrodden people live in their bungalows and Gold Coast condominiums.

But Chicago is the town that Rudyard Kipling described when he said 'I have struck a city—a real city—and they call it Chicago.' The spirit of the people that Kipling talked about—the spirit of 'I Will'—lives on today.

51 People of all shapes and sizes and ages and ethnic backgrounds gather to cheer the Cubs.

53 It's great to be alive in Chicago—especially in the spring after one of those Midwest winters.

54/55 and 56/57 Chicagoans congregate to shop at the Water Tower Place on the Magnificent Mile.

58 Jazz has always been a part of modern Chicago's life. 'Chicago Jazz' was the precursor of the Swing Era, and it was a rare jazz musician who didn't have some experience in the Windy City. Here is an outdoor gig.

59 Art lives on in Chicago, even street art.

60 The people of Chicago represent a melding of the casual with the formal, the outrageous with the staid.

61 The neighborhoods have mostly broken up, but the joys of the ethnic festival live on—a tired Italian celebrant in costume.

62 *Sometimes the living is easy.*

63 *A Chicago policewoman directing traffic on Michigan Avenue. One of our earliest memories is of the distinctive whistles that the traffic police used—quite different from the whistles of the man on the beat.*

64 *above The parks are the pride and joy of Chicago.*

64 *below Two sergeants of the Chicago Police Department exhibit the abdominal profile endemic to police sergeants all over the world.*

65 *above Happiness is being in a park.*

65 *below A vendor at Wrigley Field—the home of the Chicago Cubs, 1984 National League East Champions. For years, being a Cub fan meant always having to say you're sorry, but actually, the Cubs hold the record for the most total victories of any professional team—in any sport.*

The City of Tall Buildings

Louis Sullivan was the prophet of modern architecture, and out of his Chicago School of Architecture came many of the city's landmark buildings, those structures that revolutionized architecture the world over. The newer symbols of Chicago carried on the innovation begun by Sullivan, adding to the city's reputation as a place with unparalleled structural beauty, variety, interest and drama.

It was Sullivan, however, who was responsible for all this. He and his followers, who shared his dream of architecture as formed space, built the city. No matter how great a city is, and however abundant men, money, land and people may be, they cannot produce great architecture without the vision, imagination and genius of an artist.

But why is Chicago unique? She is not unique because she gave great architects the opportunity to rebuild a city destroyed by fire. Boston and San Francisco had also suffered great fires. And it wasn't due to the tremendously rapid increase in size and population, for New York, in common with many other American cities, grew just as rapidly. Chicago is unique in that she alone, from 1875 on, turned to great architects for her city plan and for her buildings.

Great Chicago buildings are a humane expression of a new way of life. They are humane because the architects of the Chicago School, from the first generation of the 1870s and 1880s to the present, have followed the teachings of the master, Louis Sullivan, who said, 'With me, architecture is not an art, but a religion, and that religion but a part of democracy.' In this spirit our best buildings and communities have been—and will be—designed. The love of the common man has been the glory of Chicago.

67 The John Hancock Center—100 stories that reach to a height of 1127 feet. When it was built, Chicagoans joked that it looked as if it were held together by crossed Band-aids.

69 Many of the greatest buildings in Chicago are on Wacker Drive, a double-decked boulevard that follows the southward curve of the Chicago River. Local traffic and pedestrians use the upper level and express traffic uses the lower deck.

70/71 Sears Tower (left), the world's tallest building at 1454 feet and 110 stories, a notable example of modern architecture and engineering, is on Wacker Drive.

72/73 Looking north along Michigan Boulevard. A startling panorama of giant buildings—all different architecturally—can be seen. Some of the more prominent skyscrapers are the Wrigley Building (left center, the white building), Tribune Tower (the Gothic building across the street) and, in the distance, rising above all the others, John Hancock Center.

74 right Marina City is in the distance, rising from the banks of the Chicago River.

74 left The Standard Oil Building (Standard Oil of Indiana), at 1136 feet and 80 stories, is the second-tallest structure in the city.

75 Part of the twin-tower, 60-story Marina City, when it was built, the world's tallest apartment building. Its cylindrical shape inspired many architects to copy it.

The City of Sports

Chicago has always been sports-mad. If you lived on the North Side, you were a Cub fan. If you lived on the South Side, you were a White Sox fan. If you lived on the West Side, you had a choice. In the good old days, this was true with professional football. There were the Bears on the North Side, playing in the Cubs' Wrigley Field, and the Cardinals (before they moved to St Louis) on the South Side, playing in the Sox's Comiskey Park.

Even in the days when no Chicago native had ever tried that strange sport from north of the border, the Black Hawks sold out their hockey games. And we can't forget the Bulls in basketball and the Sting in soccer.

Chicago's professional teams are loyal to the fans who support them. Most of these teams were founding members of their leagues who have stayed put, no matter what, although some disappeared simply because their leagues folded—The Chicago Rockets football team of the All America Conference, the Chicago Fire of the World Football League, the Chicago Stags of the American Basketball Association, to name a few. But tradition is the hallmark of Chicago's professional sports teams.

And there has always been plenty of non-professional sports and recreation for Chicagoans to take advantage of. If you were rich, you could play polo or sail, and, although these two sports involved amateurs, the competition was stiff—Oak Brook always did well in the United States Open polo competition, and the Chicago to Mackinac Yacht Races are legendary. But almost anyone could afford to swim at the beaches (although Lake Michigan never gets warm), ride horses in the park, ice skate, play sandlot baseball, football or soccer and generally have a good time.

77 *The sign on the front of Wrigley Field at North Clark and Addison Streets. The Chicago Cubs play in the charming second-oldest professional baseball stadium in the country.*

79 *The denizens of the outfield—The Bleacher Bums of Wrigley Field, who make life miserable for every outfielder on the visiting club.*

80 *Play Ball! A Cub pitcher lets loose.*

81 *A Cub batter awaits the pitch as thousands hold their breaths. That's still real grass, and it's played in sunshine, as baseball was meant to be played. Since the first night game in Cincinnati in 1935, the Cubs have resisted putting in lights, and Wrigley Field is the only ball park in the majors without them.*

82/83 *Wrigley Field. Although it has a seating capacity of only 37,272, it drew more than two million fans to its 81 home games in 1984.*

84 The South Side's Comiskey Park at South Shields Avenue and 35th Street—the home of the Chicago White Sox.

85 A scene at an Old Timers' Game in Comiskey Park. Willie Mays, the Hall-of-Famer of the Giants (first New York and then San Francisco) is at bat. The ball park seats 44,492.

86/87 Chicago Harbor, with its hundreds of private yacht moorings.

88 A huge sloop setting out on Lake Michigan in the Chicago to Mackinac Race. The seas can get rough on the lake— sometimes so rough that big iron-ore boats are destroyed.

89 Spinnakers straining in the wind, eager contestants set off in the Chicago to Mackinac Race.

90 A Black Hawk hockey player tries to break up a Boston Bruin shot on the Chicago goal.

91 left Equestrian events and horseback riding in general have long been popular in Chicago.

91 right Polo games at Oak Brook are of championship caliber.

92 Soldier Field, built in the Greek style—the
huge stadium where the Chicago Bears now
play their football games. It seats 64,124 for
football games, but has a capacity of
101,000.

93 *Part of the superstructure of Soldier Field.*

The City of Neighborhoods

When the great streams of immigrants arrived from foreign countries, Chicago first received the Germans and the Irish. Later came the Italians, Poles, Hungarians and Lithuanians. They settled in their own areas and thus Chicago became a city of neighborhoods. Today, the city, next to New York, has the most polyglot population in the country. Ask a Chicagoan where he is from and he might just tell you his neighborhood— Englewood, Rogers Park, Hyde Park, Lakeview.

Chicago is the largest Polish city in the world today, except for Warsaw. It is the third largest Greek city and the fourth largest Croatian city. The Luxembourgois population is large enough to support its own newspaper. There are many ethnic neighborhoods still left in the city, but they are not as sharply defined as they once were. Still, you can hear dozens of languages and eat the food of some 50 foreign countries there.

The typical adult Chicagoan didn't come from the Midwest Corn Belt and may never have seen a farm. He is probably the child or grandchild of immigrants, or even an immigrant himself. And that is why he likes his neighborhood. We have seen parents whose children moved from the North Side to the South Side weep as if they would never see them again.

When immigration to the United States was heavily curtailed in the 1920s, the number of newcomers to Chicago was greatly reduced, but following World War II, another kind of immigration began—the displaced persons. Most of these were from Europe, but there were a number of West Coast Japanese who had been interned during the war and were displaced persons in their own land. Still arriving are displaced Asians, Latin Americans, Russian Jews and Assyrian Christians.

95 *Our favorite ethnic restaurant—Zum Deutschen Eck on North Southport. Try the Koenigsberger Klopse.*

97 *Looking east along the Chicago River on St Patrick's Day. Every year the river is dyed green and then the parade starts.*

98/99 *Chicago's Chinatown goes back to late in the nineteenth century, when the Chinese who had worked laying the Western railroads began arriving in town after the Golden Spike was driven. Try this area on Chinese New Year.*

100/101 *A bus is reflected eerily in the window of a Chicago pizzeria.*

102 One downtown neighborhood is the Loop, where the elevated railroad makes its way around the rectangle of the central business district. Here is Wabash Avenue.

103 *The Biograph Theater on North Halsted Street near Fullerton. It was here in a quiet German neighborhood near DePaul University that John Dillinger was shot to death.*

The City That Works

As anyone who has ever written a book about Chicago knows, one has to include a quote from Carl Sandburg or be haled into court. Here's what he wrote about the city in 1916:

Hog butcher for the world,

Tool maker, stacker of wheat,

Player with railroads

and the nation's freight handler;

Stormy, husky, brawling,

City of the big shoulders.

It's still true, almost 70 years later, except for the hog-butcher part (the Union Stock Yards have closed).

As far as industry is concerned, Chicago is the leader in the manufacture of steel, metal products, sausages, cookies, candy, metal furniture, mattresses, envelopes, boxes, inorganic chemicals, soap, paint, gaskets, cans, saws, screws, bolts, barrels, machine tools, blowers, switchgears, radios, TVs, communications equipment, railroad equipment, surgical appliances and scientific equipment.

And that isn't all. It has more than 15,000 manufacturing plants, more than 51,000 retailers, more than 14,000 wholesalers and more than 62,000 service establishments. If Chicago, with its gross metropolitan product of almost $100 billion, were a country, it would rank tenth in the world.

Chicago never stops building. The money spent on construction is astounding. Industrial construction can run to $200 million a year, residential construction can hit $100 million and commercial construction can hit $1 billion.

Add to this the fact that Chicago is the leader in transportation with its rail centers, airports, trucking and shipping facilities, and it becomes clear that Chicago does work.

105 *Chicago is a city of huge stores and small shops—the window of a boutique on State Street (that Great Street).*

107 *An El train takes one of the curves around the corner of the Loop. Thousands of people commute to work every day on this graffitti-less public transportation.*

108 above *Chicago never stops building.*

108 below *The presses of the* Chicago Tribune *are busy all night printing some 800,000 copies of the daily paper and some 1,200,000 copies for the Sunday edition.*

109 above *Marshall Field's, one of the best, if not the best, department stores in the world, was founded in 1865.*

109 below *Chicago's O'Hare International Airport—the busiest commercial airport in the world. Some 26 airlines use the field, and there is a takeoff or landing every 45 seconds, on average. More than 50 million passengers use it per year, and three quarters of a million tons of mail and freight are handled annually. It even has the world's largest parking garage.*

The City of Lights

If Chicago is beautiful in the daytime, it becomes spectacular at night when the lights come on. At dusk, the sunset may fill the sky with red, multiplying the color in the mirrors of the skyscrapers. The shadows of these buildings lengthen as night falls. At dawn the sunrise over the lake can be almost overwhelming.

But it is between sunset and sunrise that the city becomes the city of lights. Flying over the city one can see the vast grid-shaped street plan with its major north-south and east-west thoroughfares sparkling with lights. The headlights of the cars on the streets give the whole picture a jewel-like appearance. The houses show their warm lights below and the skyscrapers are lit up in all their glory. Even the parks take on a new beauty.

Walking the streets can be a joy, especially on Michigan Avenue or State Street, where the lights of such structures as the skyscrapers and the Old Water Tower loom above and the colorful warm illumination of the shops and stores, the theaters and the restaurants can make a native proud, a visitor enthralled.

Such mammoth structures as the museums, Soldier Field and everyone's favorite piece of architecture, Buckingham Fountain, are lit up. The effect may be enchanting or almost overwhelming. But it is never dull. Every night, rain or shine, Chicago goes through yet another magnificent metamorphosis, another awe-inspiring transformation. And at no time is it more wonderful than during the Christmas season, when the decorations in homes, in store windows and on the streets enhance the holiday excitement.

111 A friendly sign in a shop window showing the outline of the Old Water Tower.

113 The splendid Buckingham Fountain in Grant Park—a night view showing its ever-changing illumination.

114/115/116 A night view from Lake Michigan of Chicago's splendid skyline.

117 Wacker Drive and the Chicago River
look like strings of jewels at night.

118 An outdoor ballet performance at night in the James C Petrillo Music Shell in Grant Park.

119 Lake Shore Drive heading toward the Loop, with the Sears Tower looming in the distance.

120/121 A night aerial view of Chicago showing the grid pattern of the street plan.

122/123 Chicago's skyscrapers at night can be almost overwhelming.